Advance Praise for *On the Desire to Levitate*:

"By turns tough, talky, triumphant, and tragic, like the Midwest itself, Alison Powell's *On the Desire to Levitate* lifts us above the lush landscapes of her vision. Hers is an elegiac imagination that, in its very lyric confidence, manages to affirm that flight is never simple—all while making it look effortless. In love with language, folk song, the raw fields, and eminence, these poems sing while conjuring. Presto!"

> —Kevin Young, poet and author of *The Grey Album*, a *New York Times* Notable Book for 2012, and Atticus Haygood Professor of Creative Writing and English at Emory University

"I've always felt that the true test of a poet lies in his/her love poems— whether to nature, god, art, the beloved, it hardly matters—for therein lies the driving force of human experience:  to release oneself from the limits of the self, to cross, as one poem puts it, "that bridge of disbelief / between who someone is and might, someday, be." The hungers of sexual experience, the imaginary heavens of child- hood, the mythic yearnings of Orpheus and Eurydice—this book abounds with examples. I suppose it goes without saying that the lyric gift required to invoke that world is an uncommon thing for any book of poems; for a first book, it is truly rare. Alison Powell's *On the Desire to Levitate* marks the beginning of a brilliant career."

> —Sherod Santos, author of *The Intricated Soul: New and Selected Poems*

"This collection celebrates the humanity and surprise of being a child, being an adult, being fully alive in this strange and perplexing and magnificent world. It's an inclusive story: angels mean something in this book, and are willing to look back at us just as hard as we look at them. Yet it's never grim—corn grows; language brims; lives rise and glow. There's often a delicious humor in this work, and always a deep and lasting integrity."

> —Charles Hood, author of *South r South.* and 2013 Hollis Summers Poetry Prize judge

On the Desire to Levitate

# The Hollis Summers Poetry Prize

GENERAL EDITOR: DAVID SANDERS

Named after the distinguished poet who taught for many years at Ohio University and made Athens, Ohio, the subject of many of his poems, this competition invites writers to submit unpublished collections of original poems. The competition is open to poets who have not published a book-length collection as well as to those who have.

Full and updated information is available on the Hollis Summers Poetry Prize web page: ohioswallow.com/poetry_prize

# On the Desire to Levitate

*Poems*

*Alison Powell*

OHIO UNIVERSITY PRESS

ATHENS

Ohio University Press, Athens, Ohio 45701
ohioswallow.com

Printed in the United States of America
Ohio University Press books are printed on acid-free paper ⊛ ™

24 23 22 21 20 19 18 17 16 15 14     5 4 3 2 1

*Library of Congress Cataloging-in-Publication Data*
Powell, Alison.
  [Poems. Selections]
  On the desire to levitate : poems / Alison Powell.
    pages cm.
  Summary: "*On the Desire to Levitate* is the first collection of poems by Alison
Powell. This striking collection includes vivid, unflinching meditations on aging,
mythology, poetry, and family. In tight, elegant lines that alternate between homage
and elegy, these poems explore known subjects with a rebellious eye: a defeated
Hercules and a bitter Eurydice, a sympathetic Lucifer, and generations of adolescent
girls as mythical adventurers moving within a beloved but confining Midwest.
Yet in Powell's skillful hands, hardship never overtakes: as judge Charles Hood
writes, "There's often a delicious humor in this work, and always a deep and lasting
integrity.""— Provided by publisher.
  ISBN 978-0-8214-2098-0 (pb) — ISBN 978-0-8214-4491-7 (pdf)
  I. Title.
  PS3616.O8796A6 2014
  811'.6—dc23

                        2014000860

# Acknowledgments

Grateful acknowledgment to the editors of the following journals in which these poems appear, sometimes in earlier versions:

*AGNI:* "Imagining Heaven" and "Lesson"
*The Antioch Review:* "Elegy for the Miner's Canary"
*Black Warrior Review:* "Shangri-La"
*Boston Review:* "After *Paradise Lost*"
*Caketrain:* "Visitor"
*Crazyhorse:* "On the Desire to Levitate" and "Darling, at the Inn"
*Denver Quarterly:* "Hylas"
*Guernica:* "Decorum: A Study"
*Meridian:* "Animals"
*New Orleans Review:* "Rogers Road"
*Phoebe:* "Florida"
*Poet Lore:* "Eminence"
*Puerto del Sol:* "Summer"
*Quarterly West:* "Elegy," "Who Knew the Water," and "In Your Teeth"
*Runes: A Review of Poetry:* "The Fields"
*Spoon River Poetry Review:* "Jeffersonville, Indiana, 1983"
*Women's Studies Quarterly:* "Flyover Country"

"Edema" appeared in *Best New Poets 2006*, Samovar Press, 2006.
"Shangri-La," "Decorum: A Study," "Edema," and "The Fields" appeared in *The Hecht Prize Anthology, 2005–2009*, Waywiser Press, 2011.

*For Alex and Sam*

# Contents

# On the Desire to Levitate

Punctuated embroidery of missteps, shoulder of the road,
steam in and out of the grates, then: *flight*. Light as a feather,
stiff as a board—down there the earth, the inflexibility. To miss

appointments. And the cleaning, the lost letters, hard
laughter and bribes. Who can stomach these parlors. Shell game
of sentences, release me from tenuous humans everywhere.

I have been a cage, and am cagey; the seething jabber,
schedules, armies, arms of madmen, make my love
of the encyclopedia and the darkened desk.

The seminary man, I do not fear him, do not
believe him. But I want to watch my words with him,
catalogue my sins to go heavenward, drunk, delighted,

electric lights bursting in the street. What strength
in silence, to lift like that, over so many Nos. A calm braided
embrace—*There she goes*. I believe nothing today, only

that the girl burned the field, the man shot his wife, the child
went deaf, the flower bloomed in the oily garage, I left,
was left, no longer left, was no longer left. *Presto*.

*I.*

# Elegy for the Miner's Canary

*Don't Go to the Mines Today*
    is a folk song, a call of premonition—
        bless the canary in the honey-

dark like a king's taster. Hard-
    hatted men releasing
        those fifty-eight devotional bones,

that soft molt. *Don't Go*
    is the premonition, is the ode
        by the bye, its wing-swift

filigree dusting the oil lamp.
    Bright bird alight, all the negative
        of echo, shadow, and gas,

rock and sharpened noir, flinging
    up to the earth at breakneck speed
        its song. Hey Hallelujah hallaloo

O yellow silk diver
    slicing that hexed air: we burn
        the bridge at both ends. We light

this fire and light ourselves with it.

# Flyover Country

We would fly over it if we could, sure enough —
each night perched up high on the barn's
tin roof, we want to be the swallows sailing over
the wheat, refuse, cul-de-sacs, and deer carcasses.

Instead we pass secrets, then shame between us
like shared liquor from corn, from moon, then
sneak back home, slide pond-wet into the coop —
rubbing the screen door hinges with spit

to make them silent. We know our home is full
of men coming out of bushes with mean things ablaze.
We see it on TV documentaries. Spooky place, home:
bestial, rank. Hours in the backyard, nights playing

light as a feather, Ouija — sometimes we see
the past and it's frightening. When we start
on talk of leaving, the whole town says it's six
in one hand, half a dozen in the other, so we sing

*I'll rock the cradle when you gone* and make the sound
of standing ovations. We do that until dawn.

# Summer

My grandfather in overalls the wild
blue of a storm sky. Me behind him
on a tractor, hands out, veering around plum
trees. Me by the beetle bag, squeezing,

the chemical smell of them. Him napping
in the carport, narcoleptic sleep, quick.
Linoleum, green beans in the kitchen,
my hands on a wooden cuckoo clock

in the bedroom or in a box of buttons. Nights
I would sneak to the cellar: jars of pickled
beets and jam, tops gray with dust. I would sit
on the stone floor before the fringed rocking

horse — its old gold eyes half-popped, broken.
Nose to metal nose, I learned the family secrets.

# Hiding and the Desire to Be Found

As a child I would tuck myself into the top shelf
of the linen closet, lightbulb at my shoulder.
I curled up in my grandmother's steamer trunk
and waited in the dark; once I pressed my hands

against the inside lid and outlined them carefully
in wide green ink. I climbed to the roof of our house,
plain in sight, unremarkable as a weather vane or bone-
breaking fall. I did this because I knew then, as now,

that each year is a black-bagged arbitrary gift.
I go on and grieve about that like a dog griever.
I wait to be found—for the door to be opened to me,
body a boomerang flung back through the opera.

When I was a child I already coveted the day.
Dear eyes: how large a space you are, how oxen free.

# Eminence

The first time I did it I was fourteen,
the boy was from Eminence: in the fields

behind the house, behind a toolshed leaning
over with turpentine, copperheads (two beagles

died that June from rooting up in those nests).
Ground was soft, grave-ground; the whole of it swept

by corn borer, tunneled in stalk. At harvest
we did it and the nights after—it crept

toward us, land felled acre by acre, shot-
holed husks. The next breakfast Mom said

"That crop's trying not to fail us—I heard it grow
last night," hands on her floured jean pockets

making me squirm. It was me she'd heard.
That surging—it hurt like hell, the devil itself.

# Shangri-La

Draw me a hangman's portrait. Draw me a fine girl
in the river. Draw me against the black of your eyes.
Draw me and what I give—lips drawn, still singing.
Draw Shangri-La, you did, did you, the year you left
with only the blues: lucky, but still. The fine girl
in the grass. We've been laid down, yes-yes, say yes,
a mouth rubbed all in tequila and sea salt, a famished
belly and you kissing it. And shadow of limestone,
and the barn, and mazes out of cornstalks. O
tanned—what legs! Inside your jeans.
Draw each thing that keeps you breathing, draw
your kitchen sink, draw a bath for coupling. My
I still love you, am drawn to your wicked ways,
to your sleepy ways, to your underwater, tiny,
sweet ways. Draw me a mouth, a red red mouth.

# Who Knew the Water

I'm calling sleep because I've been dreaming
of you with some strange drink—honey, bees' blood,
you're keeping me up all night. How your thin

shoulders, like two extinct birds, tore down
through the sun into the quarries.
How you'd hive from head to toe all over,

from dove to red. You said *shit* like *bless you*,
swan-diving off the drop-off we called Shangri-La,
palms spread and taunting. Inside that water: tools,

bottles, clothing, and leaves. What took us there:
black tie highway stretched out, ironed, calling us
to summer. Us figuring those clay and silt cradles

home, just lost enough. I miss your shoulders,
your turned unaging back. Since you stopped writing
I pretend I see you out of the corner of my eye—

they water with the ragweed wind. I'm left like this,
you planning to return as if for keys, never
to be unearthed from the couch cushions.

A gracious bowing out: your corners to stay
for me wrinkleless, your fever-yellowed, crooked
grin the same. Look, you: call. You, who've made

the pilgrimage to *forget*, think of us licking salt
off the other's wrist. Remember noon, hand slipped
between your legs like note folded into envelope;

remember sliding between fence slats,
rusted nails never claiming a knee. Even then
you knew the water would be the end of us.

# Rogers Road

In the yard there was one persimmon tree
that did nothing better than drop rot.
Her house was encased on all sides
in an aluminum caravan of cars, shadowed

and cavernous as skulls. We stretched out
on the center of the road—soft tar,
August nights—feeling electric like pale
illuminated fish. Rolling there

in the lane-split grit like eyelashes.
We were Joan of Arc on the crest of a hill;
we shared nothing in spirit or goods,
expected nothing from the present.

At a farm across the way, horses tamped
the ground to emphasize their sureness of it.

# Visitor

With you in this house, my face wears the numerous crashes
like badges. I cook and pace the floorboards, above the zoo

of vibrations from your basement music. Lolling
on the turntable, volumes of a mystery novel series.

We both have irons in the fire, each attention's divided,
we can't figure out how to tether to anything.

You land on me like a tornado, my wild barometric,
and I roll like a dog in our orange urgency.

You're a jinx. So go on, drop on by—I'll keep my distance
front and center, igloo-vested, shoulder to the wheel.

# In Your Teeth

This something I can't tell you is this:
you were born into the green broken world.
Meaning, it was already split like this,

over before you started, towel thrown
and molding. Our waitress's hands
madeleines just dusted, nerves already doing

what she calls *that upside-downness.*
Me, outside the Chinese restaurant's
garish red gates, already something

you've lost. You're not charming,
have about you a suffocating way—
indispensable, really, you.

We're two commas facing the other,
two half-finished dinners. It's easier
to offer you cowardice or my wrist

than a secret or vindictive hiss.
Vest no interest in me. Yesterday
I saw my reflection in the window,

pale and preening, while the dog and I
had another of our talks. Again I asked
*What's it you're unearthing, sweet, dumb seeker?*

She sighed. In the rose light
of the yard your postcard came,
some teeth were bared.

# Animals

Sigh and stretch tight that bridge of disbelief
between who someone is and might, someday, be.
Looks deceive. You pray that when I press your
back's hot small, I do a whole, raw thing—

do not, say, think of another's sweat, odor
of spit and sawdust. Things get cowardly;
garter snakes nest in clean barns, even
those smelling of fresh bread. I love you

exactly, I said. I lied. I know, though,
that desire to be eaten, mantis-
like, to lose your head proudly. I did once.

It was grand. A magician uncovered
a fluttering dove, it was embarrassed
by the insistent light, flew toward it.

*II.*

# The Fields

A boy is raised up in the fields.
He knows his hard feet in the husks.
He knows his mother, her bottles and naps.

Knows his brother's war dreams, is afraid
to sleep next to him. His father has a way
with the jitterbug and a whipping switch.

There are kindnesses: the giblet-
thick dressing of his grandmother,
the pictures of Venice in his schoolbook—

the gilded water. How the fathers
look in their Sunday best and the prayers,
like milk, around him.

One spring day the great god of his dreams
descends and, exploding, fills
the new tar streets with rainwater.

He inches out from under the table
where he has been reading for weeks;
he pushes out into the storm.

All around him are the old lives of leaves.
Oak tree sticks make lean-tos
without being asked, school is nowhere in sight.

Though there's water-weight to his knees,
he pokes one toe into the gutter. Here
he knows there is desperation, devotion, hard

loss. He opens his arms to the yelping sky
and cries back *Oh! Great harbor, I am
your tin ship!* before his mother, weak

in her yellow slip, yanks him inside.

# Hylas

Some days life is so slow, I envy
that your chore turned murderous

and sexual, how you went down
into the task mouth on mouth. A card

up the sleeve, a penny behind the ear—
you are famous for your disappearance.

What you sought, jaunty with that jug,
you got in spades: nymph kissing you

with one arm round your neck,
plunging you in the pool, her hunger

making its own errand. Who hasn't,
on the way to a practical task, ended up

distracted by some surprise—bad or good
or both like yours? Now you're drowned

with your urn in a cradle of arms,
sore with lovemaking and sediment.

Up here on the pedestrian globe
with its cheap battles, someone

is thinking that Dryope—having seen
the pitcher's lip slice through the surface,

seen your strong legs, that you were lost—
of course she broke from her dance

and song to sink and have you.

# The Murderer's Reverie

When I did it I made a sound that was not delight
but it was bright like that. It was not a laugh but I shook,

got lost in it. And I moved to the porch of myself
where I now live. I am afraid of children, their timeouts,

their expectant eyes, their seeking and hiding.
Could it have been another way? This way, say: I propose

in Utah where I can make her all ten of my wives.
A wedding with autoharps, a three-tier cake, her mother,

a taut white tent. People dancing like marionettes.
Sometimes I dream she's driving a tractor—I ride

shotgun, watching waves of overturned dirt.
Or I imagine a lost weekend: her waiting in a whale-

bone corset, in the clawfoot bath. Consider this curse:
he shall have a hundred houses, in those houses

a hundred rooms, and in those rooms forty beds. He shall
have a fever, be delirious, and move from bed to bed.

I am an orphanage, I live among my orphaned selves.

# Hercules Reflects on Victory

Every morsel of this world yields a groan.
Honey followed by sting, major by minor chord,

marriage vow by telegram, banquet by rape.
I had to rip the horn from a bull to win my bride.

My hands became a ring of Saturn to contract
his neck, my body became his hunchback.

I tore it from him. I tongued the gash
like an amuse-bouche. But bad begets good

begets bad. I was faithful to my wife;
her madness was more steadfast. One day

she covered me with a gasoline cloak and bid me
burn. I sat burning and it seemed no victory—

no number of whipped dogs, apples stolen,
pilgrims saved, no hollowed horn—would relieve me.

What did she want? What did I keep from her?
I end my life on earth crawling like a woman

in childbirth, trees in my teeth like a bit,
broadcast into ash and afraid of heaven.

# Eurydice

After the venom, you called as a man
with catchpenny will. With metal hunger.
One glance and I was in the hot seat again —
long drop, yanking the spines, asunder

in the same crowd of muscle, root, nonsense.
What a raw deal. There is nothing to do.
I learn another kind of language: oak
means *patience. Justice shall be done you.*

May you have nothing but echoes, reruns
of my face made see-through in this untended
land; the backward slip-'n'-slide, our gummed-
up lust. Of our bodies, I only remember

my roar, jackknife, that I was pure ricochet.
Your fidget and grin, meretricious way.

# Orpheus

You, below the avalanche, under the world:
Meretricious? I buried you so I'll take it.
Never worse off was a man. Unfurled
in you, I could talk rivers out of their way—

but what the gods predict, we execute.
Without guile I looked, pickled you in the
dark port. Now I stand hat in hand; I live
in this world of men, all war, all lark,

and I send my regrets to follow you. I send
them to their grave. What else can be done?
I go to the sirens, I kiss the waving hands.
I watch the floating opera, feel the silt.

No matter where I go here in limbo
the muteness of you extends, riotous.

# The Fall

Perhaps the oblivion of physical passion
is practice for the future and grace

of nothingness. One forgets how
hard it is to bear the hazy gentleness

of the daily routine, the in-between life,
even within the glass globe of that museum

of a Garden. What a high-wire potion it is
to let oneself play the conductor, the body

a baton; to eye the first chair and mime
the solo. They could hardly stop

themselves, that small pandemonium
of effort to hit the high note.

# After *Paradise Lost*

When the evil army comes it is accompanied
by a deceptively noble trumpet, as a woman

wears white and believes in it. An angel
is not spiteful without cause, having been flung

from the hand of God, whose engine, reportedly,
is love itself. How badly the crippled angel

wanted to be first in everything, God's
man Friday! He is not without scruple;

he envies the earth. The earth is just
beyond chaos, and so rests against chaos,

yet everything that comes from the earth's Garden
can be tended, pulled, made orderly—

blanched and laid before a guest—
the earth has something called an *offering*.

The story of the Garden is allegorical.
An allegory is like a forked tongue;

an allegory is an infant bastard who is fitful.
The Garden becomes linked with a feeling

of sickness and trepidation: a dream
of taking an air balloon ride over a river

because the bridge is burning.

*III.*

# Imagining Heaven

makes me uneasy and superstitious, so I read books
where people understand purpose and goodness
and am full of wonder. Some days, especially, I know

how impossible it is that heaven exists; I sleep
with the television on and won't leave the house
until the day is inhaled back into its sea.

As a child my imagined heaven revealed how basic
were my wants: a red porch littered with projects,
many animals, benign accidents to be tidied;

all movement like ice skating and everyone about twenty.
If there were a heaven we would be given a glimpse of it
once in a while, as we stumble over memories—

on a long drive a flash comes, we try to reel it back—
wasn't that a dream? Where was that? What a marvel,
how terrible—to have nearly lost that game, that trip,

the buttons on that dress, the grief of that cold water
on that early May morning, his room without pictures,
her jewelry box, that bowl of oranges. I can do nothing

so I put myself in the old heaven, sprawled out
on the red floor. I am youngish, the dog is with me.
I can whistle and do, having left behind this life

in New Hampshire with the car and children.

# Darling, at the Inn

*Darling, it's hot as Hades / You said it /* heat a velvet coat
draped over the bay. The conversation is impersonal:
obliging strangers at a buffet waiting for orange juice.

This unsteady mess in sweatpants, slipping jam on toast,
dreamt someone gave her a Givenchy veilless hat—blue
silk UFO—for the opera, which was silent in the dream.
There is the real above-ground life but last night

men came for her, as the hat was stolen, and there she was,
left with her face. Wet. Unusual. Many children believe all
is sleepwalk and talk, tulle and cobweb, illusion, and how not far
off they are, consider, spooning your eggs. Buttering the toast.

Above-ground there are inns and docks, slick things suspended
in a net. There are libraries with a person reaching for sweets.
But really we're being tossed like acrobats, sloppy, in our
amphitheater of machines and dreams. So you call a stranger *Dear*

or *Darling* and tell this person all sorts. What bowl you broke,
the sound it made. What creature you killed with kindness.
About your body and how later today you'll regret something else.

# Decorum: A Study

A person could be at a loss. The width, spools and yardage, meringue
airs, impossible long fingers, of decorum. Its army sashay of the side-

walk. Iguana-eyed, left on stoop, no knock or ring. The small blue bruises
from wearing these hard tasteful heels. Like molasses in a dress going

down the stairs to answer. Because to lift the unbashful marble, ah it's lit
differently, the arm would straighten. Door and doorbell taking on a low

religious typewriter drone. Stomach rot of rose milk and rubbing
alcohol. A person makes a habit of not knowing what to make of it,

as fact is, most days no door or invitation wants opening.
The table crowded with its nestled chairs. Eyes close at a glance.

# Elegy

This scab on my back is from your scattered attic,
half-moon on my palm from your funeral,

how we tucked the photos of your children
into your breast pocket. Your arms, coffined,

were barn fence; I picked up
this stutter from Grandmother, black-

clad bird. This bruise from digging
to transplant your roses—found a worm,

one tossed unraveling cigarette—and the shape
of the bed was grave plot though I didn't

mean it or stop until my lawn was half-dug.
My ears are ringing always with your cuckoo.

Sneezing from your old letters, thin as fly's wings,
and photographs: one shows your brother, arms

raised high in a forest, hands draped with snakes
like two chandeliers. When we cleared the house

I stumbled on your snakebite kit;
I broke the vial with my heel.

That whole day was end, nothing but.

# The Attic

She ate voraciously in the last days:
egoless, banging her fists on the oilcloth,

gulping the lemonade. We were so sorry
we could not put back what the invisible

thief took out. White gloves, a gentle wave,
it smeared decades of memory: names,

the regulation of hunger. All of it
whipped backward like fish on a reel

until she was like a child. I did her hair
in the home, stood awkwardly over her,

rolling gray tufts into curlers.
Her body had trailed the long-gone mind

for years, loyal as a dog; when it caught up
she was buried. It was spring. They played Taps.

There is a jar of waxy lard by the sink.
There is a jade plant in the bedroom,

the musty smell of old coats. I climb
the attic ladder and enter the pyramid—

all heat, angle, and dust. Silverfish race out
of shoeboxes as I sort through pictures:

three boys at a dance. A girl holding
a pinwheel at a fair. Their honeymoon,

a lake: she wears a striped swimsuit,
his head cocked, two ear-to-ear grins.

In another she's alone at the edge of a canyon,
arms spread wide. When I show my father

what I've found, he looks at them.
Shakes a balding head. Says *Is that right.*

Above the bed is a print of an angel,
yellow-haired, robed, ushering Hansel

and Gretel across a bridge. The woods
are blue-black, the river below bright;

the children leap toward where she points.
When my grandmother died

there was a service in the church. I read
a letter from Paul to the Thessalonians.

Then there was a reception in the basement.
My grandmother had said: *See, they follow*

*her. Because they listen, they don't get lost.*
*When they get home they sleep real hard.*

The congregation said *You take care now*
and laid out nine cherry and squash pies.

My grandfather had the greenest thumb.
My grandmother beaded another gold pillow.
My aunt wore the suede boots with fringe.
My grandfather was a boy he danced in a churchyard.
My grandfather smoked by the wood crucifix.
My grandmother took off her glasses and warned us.
My grandfather had a sweet tooth oh my oh my.
My aunt smoked thin white cigarettes.
The cookie jar said *Thou Shalt Not Steal.*
We had iced tea in the carport.
The garden had beetles by the fistful.
My grandfather had a mechanical chair.
My grandmother hotfooted it outside.
My grandfather smoked Pall Malls.
My grandfather said *You all hell-bent shoo-wee.*
We had cheese sandwiches in the living room.
My grandfather got the Jackson & Perkins catalogue.
The new hybrid teas were named Wildfire and Keepsake.
My grandfather said *Now they climb, see.*
I took the rake to the screened-in porch in summer.
I cleaned the cobwebs they fell on me.
My grandfather went up and went down.
I put salt in the sugar jar.
My grandmother said *Look there your hair.*

When I am kindest, I am asleep
in the silver hull of a rowboat
and she is rowing.

When I am kindest,
I am as good as marriage.
I am a child sunning at her feet.

# Edema

My father says *They might have to cut it off her.* Simple, like bone
and bone, her finger has fused with that old ring. She sits there,

mindless as plank wood, cawing in a starched hospice bed.
They'll use a tiny saw to do it, split the band etched near the knuckle.

Her slippered feet swell, too. Unpredictable boat-blocks, they hold
inside one move, nothing *swing,* nothing called *fox,* just one blue bee-

line, dreadful and straight. We take her wrist, crowd the bed
and we encircle her—ghost of leanness, muscle blown, skin

no more tissue than wind. This serum is serious and mean.

# Jeffersonville, Indiana, 1983

Why we are sure tired. The grocery carts, drifting pods.
Our mistakes steeped in the dull milk bath. Our worst
crop nebulous, gray, seeded. The heat. Hurry, we've run out

of each other, silent and spiteful—children from prim dumb
women, deft with scissors. The world full of butterscotch,
paper dolls around the head like a tight white crown,

brown bag chain-link garlands droop. The heat. Any minute
now. Death-defying. Plucking raisins out of carpet, knee
to shag. Morning, glass and phone, morning oh my,

watch and sewing, tomato pincushion red breast, mis-
carriage. Why was that the doorbell. It was such grace,
heard from inside this fireplace. What precision.

This sticky toothed heat, willows, locusts. My what
empty. What lapping shadowy strides. Shuffleboard sand,
here's to a speedy recovery, patent leather shoes like a fist.

# Florida

*Girl, get up with me on this here couch.*
She is angry and soiled, thin. Perfumed

with smoke, urine and liquor. Liver-spotted
like a cheetah and half-bald. The bottom row

won't hold so she's half-teethed, laughs
at nothing or wrong things. There are stairs

here that we insist she does not climb, because
her legs are paper mache and she's wined up good

by eleven. In this panhandle pink shell
of a tomb, we don't get her started on men.

She waits to be in her wood box, divinely
sullen—we can say it's so because

she tells us so. *Girl, here, have a chocolate.*
We stain ourselves, furtive with melted sweets.

Rotted root on the davenport, she curls,
solicitous, toward us. Deep in the settled porch,

eighty and hot and sleepy. Her cigarette smoke
envelops us within the mesh walls. Through this

screen's screen, I see overripe orange trees—
she says *Right free for the taking.* There are hawks—

she spits, says *Crows,* rustling her face. Turns
the hollows of her eye sockets straight at us,

dares us to comment on the coming storm.
She watches the neighbor man come

and go breezily, with his lover. On this
she has much delirious comment.

Late in the afternoon, there is a ringing
inside—a telemarketer is calling—

and she hears the phone over the fitful wind
before my mother or me. She hears,

well and far. My mother *oohs* and *ahs,* coos
over her mother's ears—those ancient, jeweled

lobes, those red intact drums. *This is your
inheritance,* my mother whispers, pleased

with the genes, cracking a walnut,
squeezing the silver pliers.

# Lesson

When I imagine aging further, I salivate and fidget,
want to strip or argue hard, fry something, spin.

Each day my body gains something and loses,
so I do things for the sake of it, am a woman smiling

at her enemy at the party. To keep me company,
I search for someone to paint into my corner—

together we'd shrink from the passing ambulance,
disbelieving, forgiven as dogs. My mother,

with her one way to age, her giving in, glides
through hollow rooms. Her house a white sure drum,

the television echoes. She says she dreams of nothing,
calls dreaming voodoo; between quilt stitches,

her looks reward me nothing. No one touches her
while she prepares her wholesome meals,

hummingbirds circle the impenetrable place,
ignored. When I am old I know the days might stare

like sharks, open mouthed, waiting for the glint.
My mother taught me to nap. In the middle

of each day, in separate poised ways,
we lie on our beds and wait.

My humble gratitude to the following friends, teachers, and colleagues whose comments on this manuscript or individual poems was especially helpful: Simeon Berry, Catherine Bowman, Charles Hood, Marie Howe, Emily Raabe, David Sanders, Sherod Santos, Mary Speaker, David Wojahn, and Kevin Young. Special thanks to poets and friends Steve Gehrke, Micah Ling, and Jennifer Scaife for their advice when this manuscript was in its last stages. I am particularly indebted to poet Jessica Garratt for her generous feedback and advice. Most of all, I am deeply grateful to my parents, Ron and Frona; my brother, Aaron; and my aunt Grace Hamilton for their steady support and kindness.

Thanks to the Department of English at Indiana University, University of Missouri, CUNY Graduate Center, Fine Arts Work Center of Provincetown, Vermont Studio Center, and Writers @ Work for their generous support during the writing of this book, and to Ohio University Press for offering it a home. Thank you to Suzanne Koett, the artist responsible for the cover image, and to Mary Speaker, who designed the cover.

Finally, this book is dedicated to my husband, Alex, who changed everything, and my son, Samuel, who did it again.